This book belongs

The Very Interesting Life of The Chevalier de Saint-Georges by Mrs. Judy Naillon "ViolinJudy"
Copyright © 2023 ViolinJudy
www.violinjudy.com
ISBN: 978-1-960674-17-3

Joseph Bologne,
who was later known as the Chevalier de
Saint-Georges, was born on
Christmas Day, December 25th, 1745.

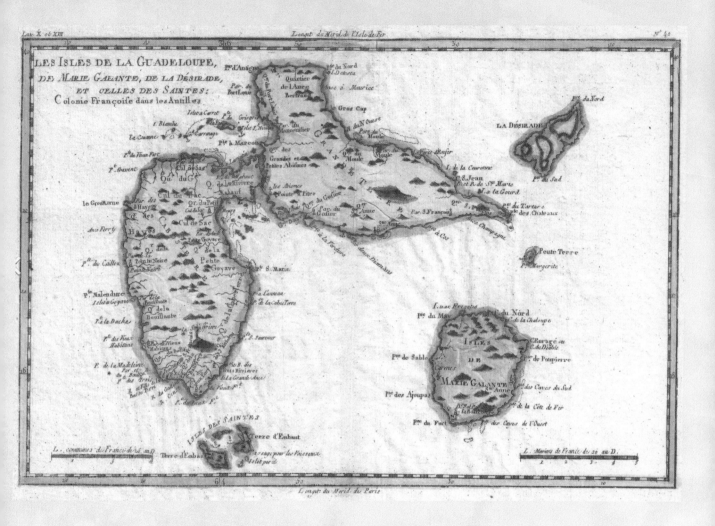

He was born in Baillif, Guadeloupe which is an island in the Caribbean near where Haiti is today.

Joseph's dad was French and a plantation owner where they grew sugar cane and coffee beans. Joseph's mom, Nanon was a slave owned by his father. Many people said she was the most beautiful woman on the island.

Joseph's dad really loved him and did not want him to be treated like a slave. He wanted Joseph to be baptized, and to have an education. When Joseph was seven his father took him to a boarding school in France, left him there, and went back to the island. How do you think Joseph felt?

Two years later Joseph's parents Georges and Nanon came to France. They moved to a nice apartment in Paris.

Joseph's dad became a Gentleman of the King's Chamber in 1757. This means King Louis XV gave his dad a title- kind of like a new name, that made him more important and well known.

King Louis XV also known as
"Louis the Well-Beloved"

In France Joseph was able to attend school, have music lessons, horse riding and dancing lessons and learn sports like fencing in the picture below. He also became an excellent swimmer!

Joseph was quick to learn and became very good at almost everything he tried
He also learned to play the violin!

In France, Joseph was treated much better than when he was a slave in Guadeloupe! However he and his mom still didn't have freedom. In France they had to abide by "Les Codes Noirs" which were laws in France that restricted the lives of people of color. This means Joseph was treated differently-worse-because of his skin color.
He was also not able to inherit his father's titles.

When Joseph was 13 he attended the
Royal Academy, where he learned
fencing and horsemanship.

Joseph's fencing teacher, Nicolas Texier de la Boëssière was excellent and taught him everything he knew. A rival fencing master named Picard once insulted Joseph so Joseph challenged him to a dual! They fenced each other in front of a large crowd! Even though Joseph was young, he won the match! His dad was so pleased that he bought his son a horse and carriage!

In just a few years Joseph was a champion fencer and accomplished horseman. People described his arms as being "faster than lightning". Joseph fought many duels and matches in France and England. He was also well liked, smart, charming and handsome. He became well-known, and had many friends and invitations to dinner!

When Joseph graduated in 1766 he was knighted by the king and made a a *Gendarme du roi* (Officer of the King's bodyguard) and a chevalier, which is a member of orders of knighthood. Now Joseph was known as as the 'Chevalier de Saint-Georges'.

Henry Angelo, who ran a famous fencing academy in London, wrote of Saint-Georges that: "Never did any man combine such suppleness with so much strength. He excelled in every physical exercise he took up, and was also an accomplished swimmer and skater ... He could often be seen swimming across the Seine with only one arm, and in skating his skill exceeded everyone else's. As to the pistol, he rarely missed the target. In running he was reputed to be one of the leading (athletes) in the whole of Europe".

Everyone was talking about the new Chevalier de Saint-Georges! Now famous, he was known as a great athlete, fist fighter and fencer. Many called him "the god of arms" which meant he was the best at fencing and shooting.

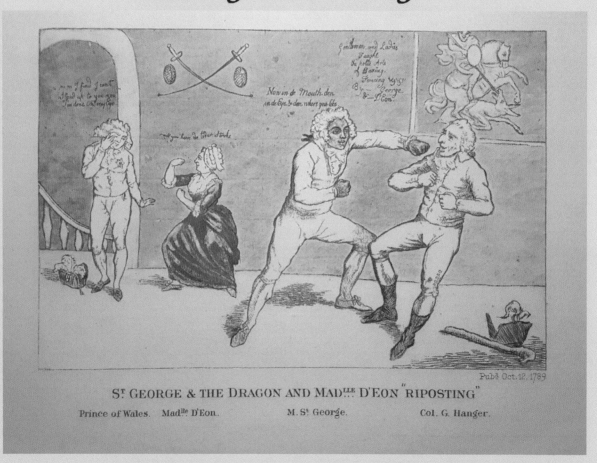

ST. GEORGE & THE DRAGON AND MAD.ᴸᴸᴱ D'EON "RIPOSTING"

Prince of Wales.   Mad.ˡˡᵉ D'Eon.   M. Sᵗ George.   Col. G. Hanger.

A cartoon of the Chevalier fencing with Colonel Hanger captioned "St. George & the Dragon" appeared in the Newspaper "The Morning Post" on April 12, 1789.

Saint-Georges was also an excellent musician and surprised many people in Paris in 1769 when he played solo violin in a concert. Even more surprising was that he had composed (written) the pieces himself!

Later, he became the concertmaster (the leader and best player) of the orchestra which was the largest symphony orchestra in the world! He conducted the world premier of Haydn's six "Paris Symphonies." He began composing (writing) music for the orchestra to play and became the conductor of the orchestra.

Franz Joseph Haydn, who composed the Paris Symphonies

In 1776 the Chevalier de Saint-Georges was recommended for an even better job as the director of the Paris Opera! However three of the leading ladies took a petition to Queen Marie Antoinette saying they wouldn't take orders from Joseph because he was "mixed race." This means his parents had different skin colors.

The Paris Opera House

Joseph knew the queen and didn't want to embarrass her so he declined the job. However, now Queen Marie Antoinette invited Joseph to play music with her and just a few other musicians! We can guess that she played the piano while he played the violin. The queen later invited Saint-Georges to perform with her on stage at the royal palace, in what many people considered an apology.

The Chevalier de Saint-Georges was honored to have such an important friend in Queen Marie Antoinette, however many people were jealous of his fame and good luck and spread rumors about him.

A year later Joseph wrote his first opera called *Ernestine*, however after the premiere it was not performed again–it had bad reviews. The critics had liked his music but not the words, which were written by someone else. He wrote more operas and was invited to live with the Duke of Orléans in 1780. He served as the Duke's Lieutenant of the Hunt and was also the Music Director of the Duke's wife's theatre. This is where his third opera was performed.

In 1789 the French Revolution began. Now Joseph decided to enlist in the Revolutionary Army, which fought for liberty and equality. Three years later a calvary of volunteers from the West Indies and Africa was founded and Joseph was the colonel. It was the first all-black army regiment in Europe and Joseph was such a great leader that everyone started calling the soldiers the Légion Saint-Georges. There were over 1,000 men under his command.

Some people didn't think that the Chevalier should succeed because of his skin color. Soon after he was made a colonel in the army he was accused of using military money to pay his own debts. However he soon was found innocent (that means he didn't do it!)
Another time he was dismissed from the army and put in prison for 18 months, but released and no case was brought against him. This means he may have been put in prison for no reason!
Others said he shouldn't write or perform music during a war.
The Chevalier finally was able to return as colonel of his regiment but now there were two other colonels and he wasn't needed.

In 1797 Chevalier de Saint-Georges returned to Paris and became director of a new orchestra called "The Circle of Harmony" and it performed in the former residence of the Duke of Orléans. The Chevalier dedicated himself to being an excellent violinist and musician.

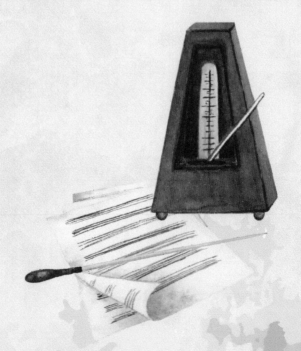

On June 10, 1799, Joseph Bologne, the Chevalier de Saint-Georges, died of bladder disease. He was 53 years old and was buried at the "Temple of Liberte and Egalite" which is now called the Church of St. Marguerite.

Many of his works were lost during the French Revolution and forgotten but today we remember him as one of the earliest classical composers of mixed race and African ancestry, as well as an excellent military leader, sportsman and musician.

We still celebrate, play and listen to music by the Chevalier of Saint-Georges today!

MONSIEUR DE St GEORGE.

There are many memorials to the Chevalier de Saint-Georges and one is this Paris street which was named the "Rue de Chevalier de Saint-Georges" in his honor.

More Very Interesting Joseph Bologne Facts:

President John Adams wrote that Chevalier de Saint-George was "the most accomplished man in Europe."

———————◦◦◦◦◦◦———————

One of the officers under his command was named Thomas-Alexandre Dumas, future general-in-chief in the French army and father of the author of the famous book *The Three Musketeers.*

———————◦◦◦◦◦◦———————

Mozart, who was born twenty years after Joseph Bologne definitely met and knew him! During the summer of 1788, Bologne was living at the Duke of Orlean's mansion. The Duke's personal secretary also lived there, and that summer the secretary invited a guest of his own: Wolfgang Amadeus Mozart! So for a few months, the two great musicians lived at the same address!

Some people call Le Chevalier de Saint-Georges "The Black Mozart" however the Chevalier was born twenty years before Mozart and famous long before Mozart was even born!

Mozart was having a hard time in life; sad, lonely, learning a new language and trying to get people to pay him for work he had completed. He met the Chevalier Saint-Georges who was handsome, smart, famous, at ease, popular with the ladies and even close friends with the Queen. While we don't have proof it is easy to imagine Mozart would have been jealous, and perhaps why the two didn't become friends. Also, the Chevalier conducted one of the best orchestras in Europe while Mozart's symphonies were performed by less qualified musicians.

The Chevalier's fencing teacher La Boessiere, was a legendary fencing instructor who is credited with inventing the fencing mask. Saint-Georges became an exceptional fencer and boxer. La Boessiere left behind a number of statements attesting to his phenomenal athletic prowess.

"Perhaps the most extraordinary man to appear in the history of fencing as well as in all other physical accomplishments."

"Nature made him and then broke the mold"

"[At age 15] "he was beating the strongest fighters. At 17 he acquired the greatest speed"

The only thing that really managed to slow down the Chevalier's fencing career was an injury to his Achilles' heel, which happened while he was dancing, and probably dancing very well!

Rue Saint-André-des-Arts 49 where Saint-Georges lived.

About the Author:

Mrs. Judy Naillon or "ViolinJudy" is a dedicated and enthusiastic independent piano and violin teacher, composer, and professional violinist. Her work consists of her large private music studio as well as playing with her string quartet, and she served as a church musician for over 15 years. She has been a symphony violinist for over twenty years.

You can find more of her books at:
www.ViolinJudy.com

Printed in Great Britain
by Amazon

28203942R00021